# Tongue Twisters
～英語の早口言葉～

**CD-88**

**Double bubble gum
bubbles double.**

2倍の風船ガムは2倍にふくらむ。

**CD-89**

**I scream, you scream,
We all scream, for ice cream!**

わたしがさけんで、あなたがさけんで、
みんなでさけぶよ、アイスクリーム！

# CONTENTS もくじ

この本の使い方　4

**Nice to Meet You!**
はじめまして！　5

### Unit 1
**Alphabet Jingle & Chant**
アルファベットでお口のたいそう　6

### Unit 2
**Color Your Outfits**
洋服はどんな色？　8

### Unit 3
**This is My Family**
ミサの家族しょうかい　10

### Unit 4
**Who Says Oink, Oink?**
だれの鳴き声かな？　12

### Unit 5
**Fruits & Vegetables**
くだものと野菜さがし　14

### Unit 6
**Numbers & Shapes Maze**
数字と形のめいろへようこそ　16

### Unit 7
**Jump Rope Rhymes**
なわとび歌で遊ぼう　18

### Unit 8
**Toys Spot the Difference**
クリスマスまちがいさがし　20

### Unit 9
**Shopping List Code**
買い物に行こう　22

### Unit 10
**Sing & Draw Vehicles**
のりもの絵かき歌　24

### Unit 11
**Origami Newspaper**
新聞で折り紙をしよう　26

**Unit 12**
## The School Sugoroku
学校すごろくで遊ぼう　28

**Unit 13**
## Vacation Mix-Up
海や山で何して遊ぶ？　30

**Unit 14**
## Friends & Feelings
気持ちをあらわす言葉　32

**Unit 15**
## Homes of Wild Animals
動物たちのふるさと　34

**Unit 16**
## Cooking Bingo
今日のごはんは何かな？　36

**Unit 17**
## Misa's Garden Story
庭で野菜ができるまで　38

**Unit 18**
## Sports Dot-to-Dot
スポーツ大好き　40

**Unit 19**
## Rhyming House
家の中でライミング　42

**Unit 20**
## Follow Your Dream
大人になったら何になる？　44

**Unit 21**
## Misa's One Fine Day
ミサの一日　46

**Unit 22**
## Storytelling
カエルの王子様　48

ゲームの手引きとCDスクリプト　50

答えのページ　62

## この本の使い方

この本には、英語の文字で楽しく遊べるゲームがたくさん入っているよ。
CDを聞きながらゲームで遊べば、英語がどんどん楽しくなるよ。

※CDで合図の音が聞こえたら、一時停止ボタンを押してね。

**設問**
このマークのところにゲームの内容が書いてあるよ。

**歌**
いっしょに英語の歌を歌ってね。

**答え**
ゲームができたら、このページを見て答え合わせをしよう。

**トラック番号**
CDの、この番号のところを聞きながら遊んでね。

英語のはじめはABC。
ぼくたちといっしょに、リズムに合わせて
アルファベットを大きな声で言ってみよう。

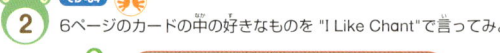

（この紙面は見本です）

**チャンツ**
CDに合わせて、リズムよくチャンツを言ってみよう。

**All About Me**
🧑 や 🧍 のところに、自分についてのいろいろなことを絵でかいて、言ってみよう。

# Nice to Meet You!

## はじめまして！

Hi. I'm Froggy.
What's your name?
やぁ。ぼくはフロギーだよ。
あなたの名前は？
いっしょに英語のゲームで遊ぼうね。

Hello.
My name is Misa.
こんにちは。
わたしの名前はミサです。
みんなとお友だちになりたいな。

CD-01

This book belongs to _____ .

お父さん・お母さんに手伝ってもらって
自分の名前を書いてみよう。

にがお絵

# Unit 1
# Alphabet Jingle & Chant
## アルファベットでお口のたいそう

**1** ミサといっしょに "The ABC Song" を歌おう。

 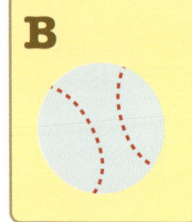    

 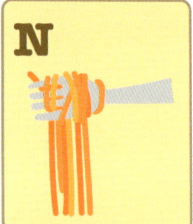    

 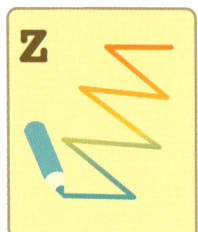

A〜Zのカードの絵を見ながら、
"The Alphabet Jingle" を言ってみよう。

英語のはじめはABC。
ぼくたちといっしょに、リズムに合わせて
アルファベットを大きな声で言ってみよう。

## 2 　6ページのカードの中の好きなものを "I Like Chant" で言ってみよう。

Which is your favorite picture card?

H, 🐴. H, H, 🐴.

M, 🐵. M, M, 🐵.

**All About Me**　あなたはどのカードが好き？
1つ選んで文字と絵をかいて言ってみよう。

〇, ▢. 〇, 〇, ▢.

seven 7

# Unit 2
# Color Your Outfits
### 洋服はどんな色？

**1** CD-05 ミサといっしょに洋服をさがして色をぬってね。（答えは62ページ）

It's red.

What color is your hat?

明日はミサのおじいさんのおたんじょう日。
ミサはパーティーにどんな洋服を
着ていくのかな？

 **2** CD-06 "Mary is Wearing"をかえ歌で歌おう。

All About Me　あなたの好きな洋服の色をぬって、かえ歌を歌ってみよう。

nine 9

# Unit 3
# This is My Family
## ミサの家族しょうかい

 **CD-07**

**1** ミサのヒントを聞いて、ミサの家族をゆびさしてみてね。（答えは62ページ）

Who is this woman?

That is my mother.

ミサのおじいさんのおたんじょう会。
親せきがたくさん集まっているよ。
どれがミサの家族かな？

**All About Me**　CD-08

あなたの家族のひとりの絵をかいて、
しょうかいしてみよう。

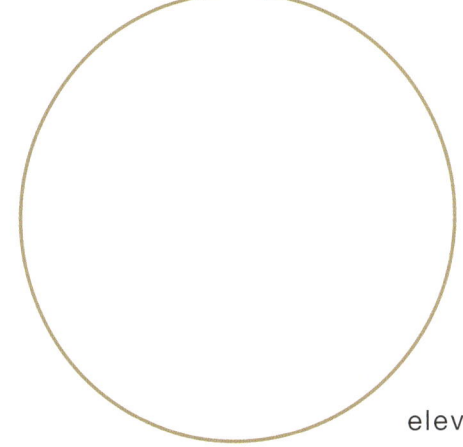

## Unit 4
# Who Says Oink, Oink?
### だれの鳴き声かな？

**1** "Old MacDonald Had a Farm"を歌いながら、めいろを通ってゴールまで行こう。歌に出てくる動物に会えるかな？

（答えは62ページ）

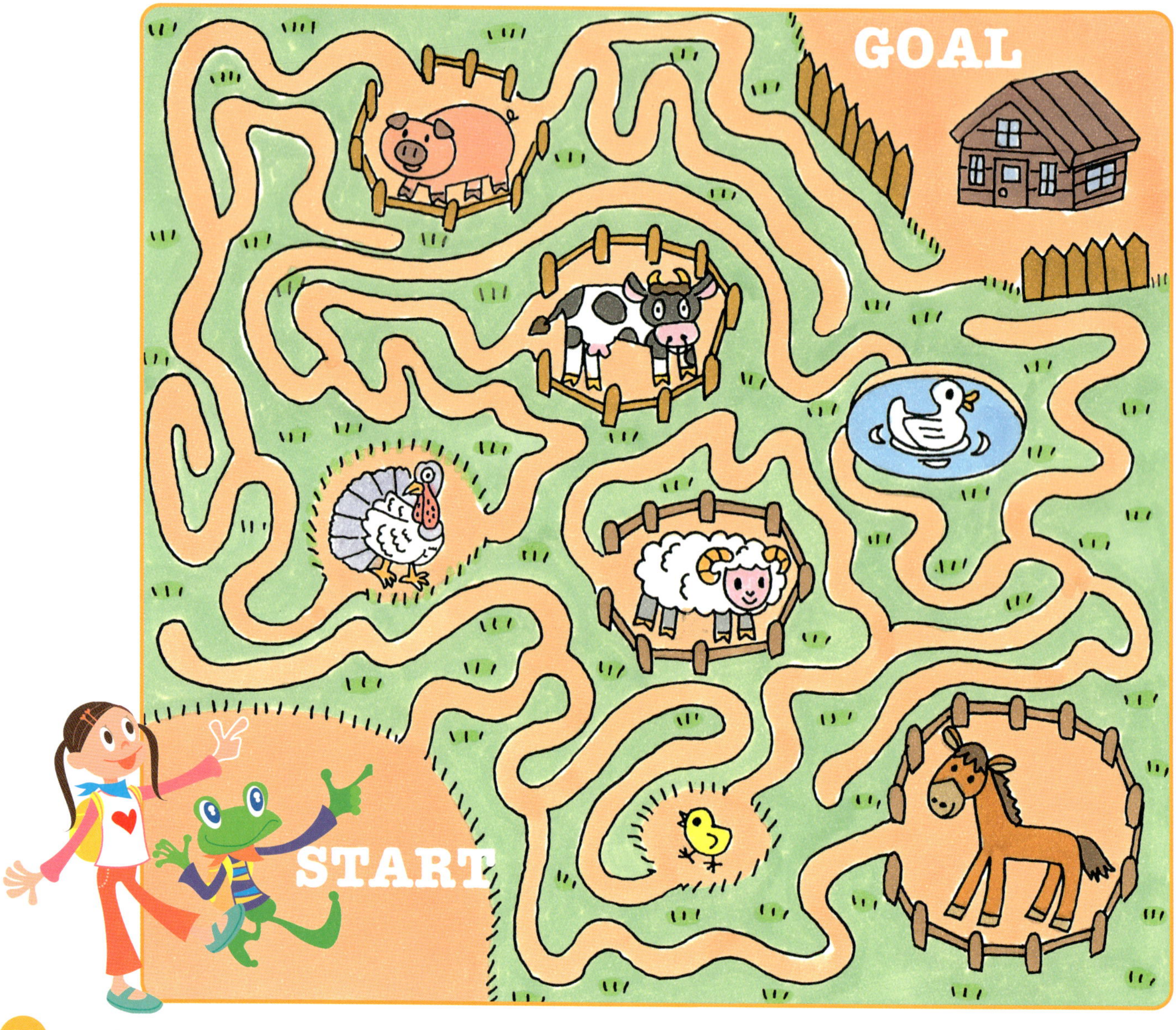

ミサは農場に遊びに来たよ。
いろいろな動物がいるね。
耳をすまして動物たちの鳴き声を聞いてみよう。

**2** CD-11 だれの鳴き声か当ててね。答えは1〜30まで点を結んだらわかるよ。

（答えは62ページ）

Do you have any pets?

Yes, I have a dog.

**All About Me** CD-12 あなたのペット・かいたいペットの絵をかいて言ってみよう。

# Unit 5
# Fruits & Vegetables
## くだものと野菜さがし

 **CD-13**

かくれている8種類のくだものと8種類の野菜を見つけよう。

くだものや野菜がどこでとれるか、
みんなは知っているかな？
ぼくが英語で教えてあげるよ。

"Fruit & Vegetable Chant"で答え合わせをしよう。（答えは62ページ）

あなたの好きなくだもの・野菜は何かな？　絵をかいて言ってみよう。

What fruits and vegetables do you like?

I like 　, 　, 　 and 　.

I like 　, 　, 　 and 　.

fifteen 15

# Unit 6
# Numbers & Shapes Maze
## 数字と形のめいろへようこそ

**1** CD-16 CD-17

三角形だけをたどってゴールをめざそう。
宝箱のところにきたらCDを聞いて、計算問題をといてね。

Q1  1+☐=☐
Q2  2☐5=☐
Q3  6☐2=☐
Q4  8☐☐=☐

CD-18
計算問題の答え合わせをしよう。
（答えは62ページ）

16 sixteen

数字と形のめいろに
ミサがまよいこんでしまったよ。
ミサをゴールまで連れていってあげてね。

**2** "Twinkle, Twinkle, Little Star"を歌いながら□☆○を数えてみてね。

（答えは62ページ）

 自分についての数字を答えてね。表に絵や数字をかきこんで言ってみよう。

**How old are you?**

**I'm eight years old.**

| | ⑧ | | ③ |
|---|---|---|---|
| |  |   123-0987 |  |
|  Me |   ○ |  |  ○ |

seventeen 17

# Unit 7
# Jump Rope Rhymes
## なわとび歌で遊ぼう

**1** 歌いながらなわとびをしてみよう。

Misa, can you jump rope?

Yes, I can.

---

**ひとりなわとび（なん回とべるかな？）** CD-21
**Alphabet Soup**

A, B, C in the .

What will I find in the ?

A, B, C, D, E, F, G, H, I, J, K, L, M, N, O,

P, Q, R, S, T, U, V, W, X, Y, Z.

---

**ひとりなわとび** CD-22
**I Love Coffee**

I love ,

I love .

I love ,

And  love me!

英語にもたくさんのなわとび歌があるよ。みんなもなわとび歌を覚えて、お友だちと外で遊んでみよう。

## 大なわとび　Teddy Bear

とびながら■のところで同じ動きをしてみよう。　CD-23

 ,  ,  .  ,  .

 ,  ,  .  ,  ,  .

 ,  ,  .  ,  ,  .

 ,  ,  .  ,  ,  .

 All About Me　CD-24

あなたはいくつできるかな？　できるものには○をつけて言ってみよう。

 ○　○　○　✕　○

# Unit 8
# Toys Spot the Difference
## クリスマスまちがいさがし

**1** CD-25 CD-26

AとBの絵には6つのちがいがあるよ。
"Jingle Bells"を歌いながら見つけてね。

**2** CD-27

ミサたちといっしょに答え合わせをしよう。（答えは62ページ）

クリスマスイブの夜。
ミサの家にサンタクロースがやって来たよ。
ミサはどんなプレゼントをもらうのかな。

How many presents are there?

B

Eleven.

# Unit 9
# Shopping List Code
## 買い物に行こう

**1** CD-28 ♪ "I'm Going to the Store"をミサが歌っているよ。
ミサはどこで何を買うのかな？

Where are you going, Misa?

I'm going to the bookstore.

**Shopping List**
1.
2.
3.
4.
5.
6.

**2** CD-29 ♪ ミサが何を買うか、わかったかな？　答えを聞いてみよう。　（答えは62ページ）

これからミサと買い物に行くところだよ。
おや、ミサの買い物リストにはふしぎな絵が
かかれているね。

（答えは62ページ）

**3** どこで何が買えるかな？　買い物リストの順にお店をまわってみよう。

**All About Me**　CD-30

あなたの好きなお店をかいて言ってみよう。

# Unit 10
# Sing & Draw Vehicles
## のりもの絵かき歌

 **CD-31**

**1** 絵かき歌を歌いながら、点線をなぞってのりものの絵をかいてみよう。

**CD-32**
  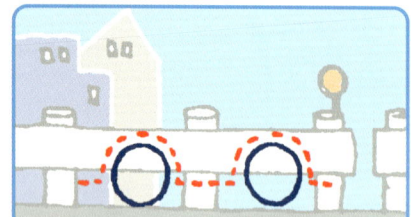

**CD-33**

**CD-34**

**All About Me** **CD-35**

自分でも絵かき歌をつくってみよう。

みんなはどんなのりものが好きかな？
絵かき歌を歌いながら、いろいろなのりものの絵をかいてみよう！

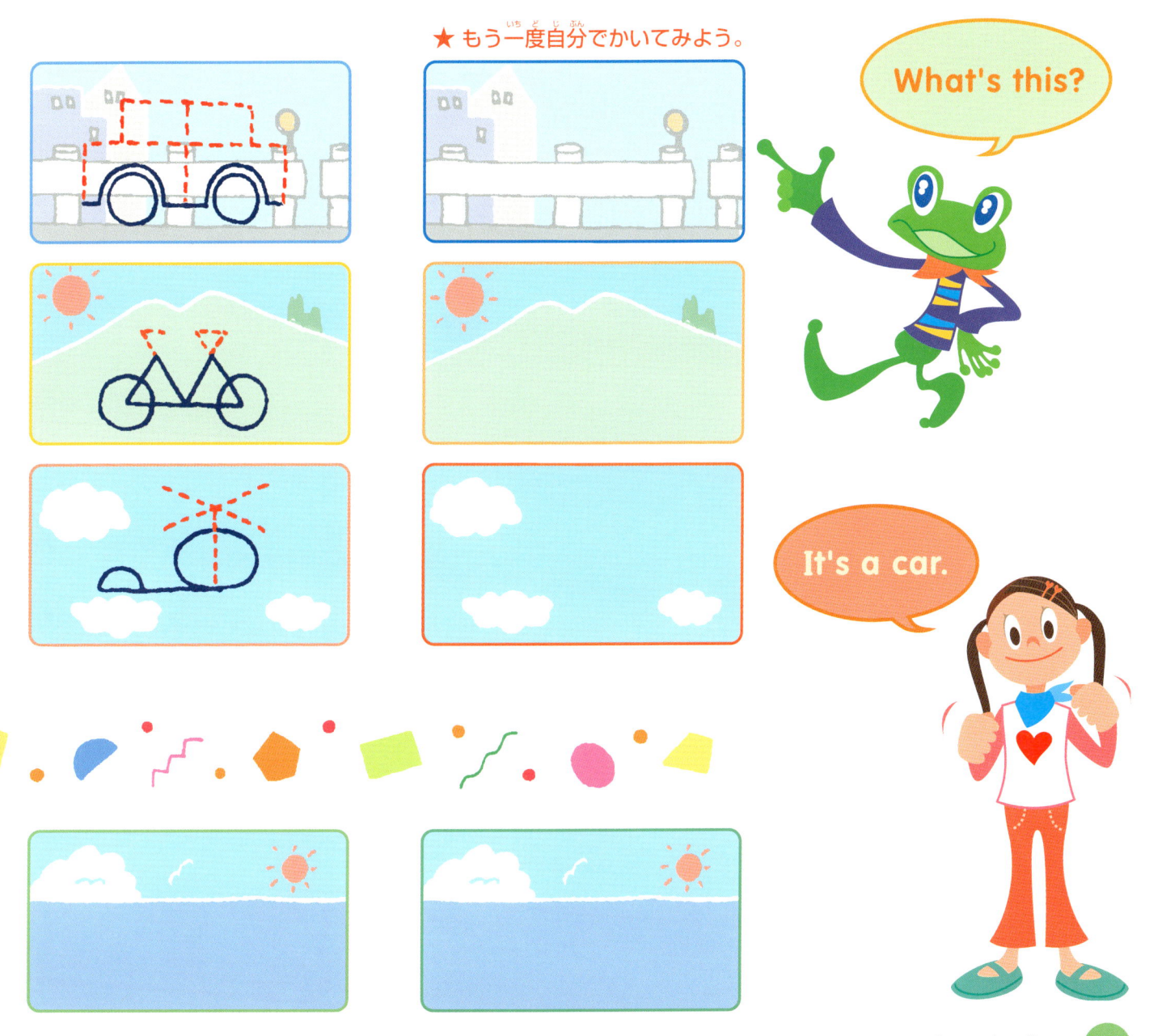

★ もう一度自分でかいてみよう。

What's this?

It's a car.

twenty-five 25

Unit 11

# Origami Newspaper
## 新聞で折り紙をしよう

CD-36

英語を聞きながら、日本のかぶととアメリカのぼうしを折ってみよう。

How do you make Kabuto?

First, fold the newspaper.

かぶと　Kabuto

1　2　A
3　4　5
6 B　7 C　D　Dを内側に折りこむ

新聞で作るぼうしの折り方を英語で聞いてみよう。
日本とアメリカでは形がちょっとちがうようだね。

CD-37

ぼうし　Newspaper Hat

CD-38

2 英語でマジックにちょうせんしてみよう。何ができるかわかるかな？
（答えは62ページ）

# Unit 12
# The School Sugoroku
## 学校すごろくで遊ぼう

ミサは学校でどんな一日をすごしているのかな？
みんなはどうかな？
学校の一日をすごろくで遊ぼう！

GOAL

Go to Teachers' room. Miss a turn.

CD-44 English

Social Studies
CD-47

Recess Go back 2.

CD-46 PE

CD-45 Music

All About Me  CD-48
あなたはどの教科が好き？　○をつけて言ってみよう。

**What's your favorite subject?**

**My favorite subject is English.**

Me

Unit 13
# Vacation Mix-Up
## 海や山で何して遊ぶ？

 **CD-49**

**1** 海と山の絵のおかしなところを8つずつさがして言ってみよう。

**CD-50** **CD-51**

CDを聞いてたしかめてみよう。（答えは63ページ）

thirty

夏休み。ミサは海へ、ぼくは山へ遊びに行くよ。
あれあれ、下の2つの絵には何かおかしなところがあるね。

What's wrong?

A polar bear is on the beach.

# Unit 14
# Friends & Feelings
## 気持ちをあらわす言葉

"Let's Make a Face"を歌おう。

Let's make a face, a ,  face.

 ,  ,  and  . 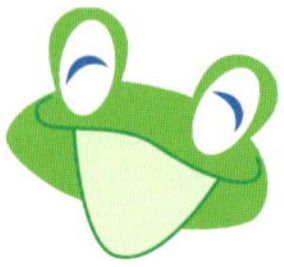  !

Let's make a face, a , 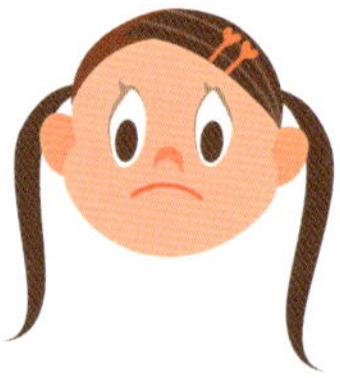  face.

 ,  ,  and .  !

Let's make a face, a , 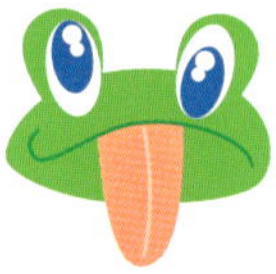  face.

 ,  ,  and .  !

Are you happy?

Yes, I'm happy.

気持ちをあらわす英語の言い方はたくさんあるよ。うれしい時やかなしい時はどう言ったらいいのかな？

## 2 CD-53
いろいろな気持ちを言ってみよう。

## 3 CD-54
ぼくたちはどんな時、どんな気持ちになるでしょう？
アメリカと日本の顔文字のちがいも見てね。　（答えは63ページ）

## All About Me  CD-55
あなたはどんな時、どんな気持ち？　絵をかいて言ってみよう。

thirty-three  33

# Unit 15
# Homes of Wild Animals
動物たちのふるさと

**1** CD-56 〜 CD-62  3つのヒントを聞いて動物を当ててね。（答えは63ページ）

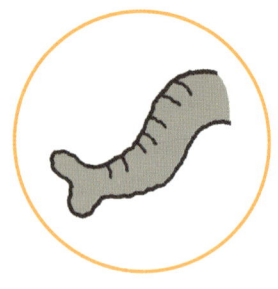

動物園にいる動物たちにも
それぞれふるさとがあるよ。
動物たちは世界のどこから来ているのかな？

Where are koalas from?

They are from Australia.

**All About Me** CD-63

地図の中から動物を1つえらんで、3ヒントクイズをつくってみよう。

thirty-five

## Unit 16

# Cooking Bingo
### 今日のごはんは何かな？

**1** CD-64 CD-65 　フロギーの"Food Chant"に合わせて、ミサとビンゴで遊んでみよう。

**遊び方**

1 カバーの絵を切りとって…（コピーしてもいいよ）

2 それをならべよう。

みんなは朝ごはんに何を食べたい？
いろんな料理の名前をぼくたちとビンゴで
遊んで覚えよう。

**All About Me**  CD-66

あなたは朝、昼、夜に何を食べたい？　絵をかいて言ってみよう。

**What do you like to eat for breakfast?**

**I like to eat toast.**

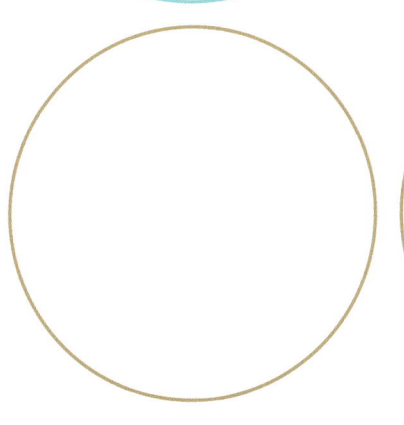

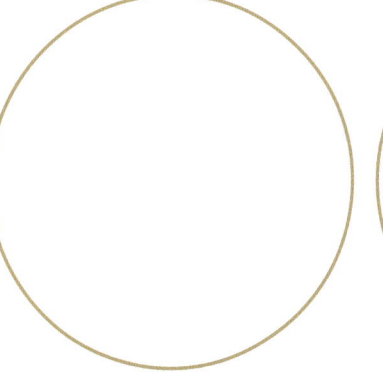

thirty-seven

# Unit 17
# Misa's Garden Story
## 庭で野菜ができるまで

**1** CD-67 フロギーといっしょに
"Oats, Peas, Beans, & Barley Grow"を歌おう。

CD-68 お話を聞いてみよう。

ミサの野菜づくりのお話をぼくがつくったよ。
ミサは庭でどんな野菜を
育てていたのかな。

What are you doing?

I am watering the seeds.

（答えは63ページ）

**2** CD-69 "Story Chant"で聞こえた順に、絵に番号をつけよう。

# Unit 18
# Sports Dot-to-Dot
## スポーツ大好き

**1** CD-70 Aから順に点を結んでみよう。同じスポーツの道具が見つけられるかな？

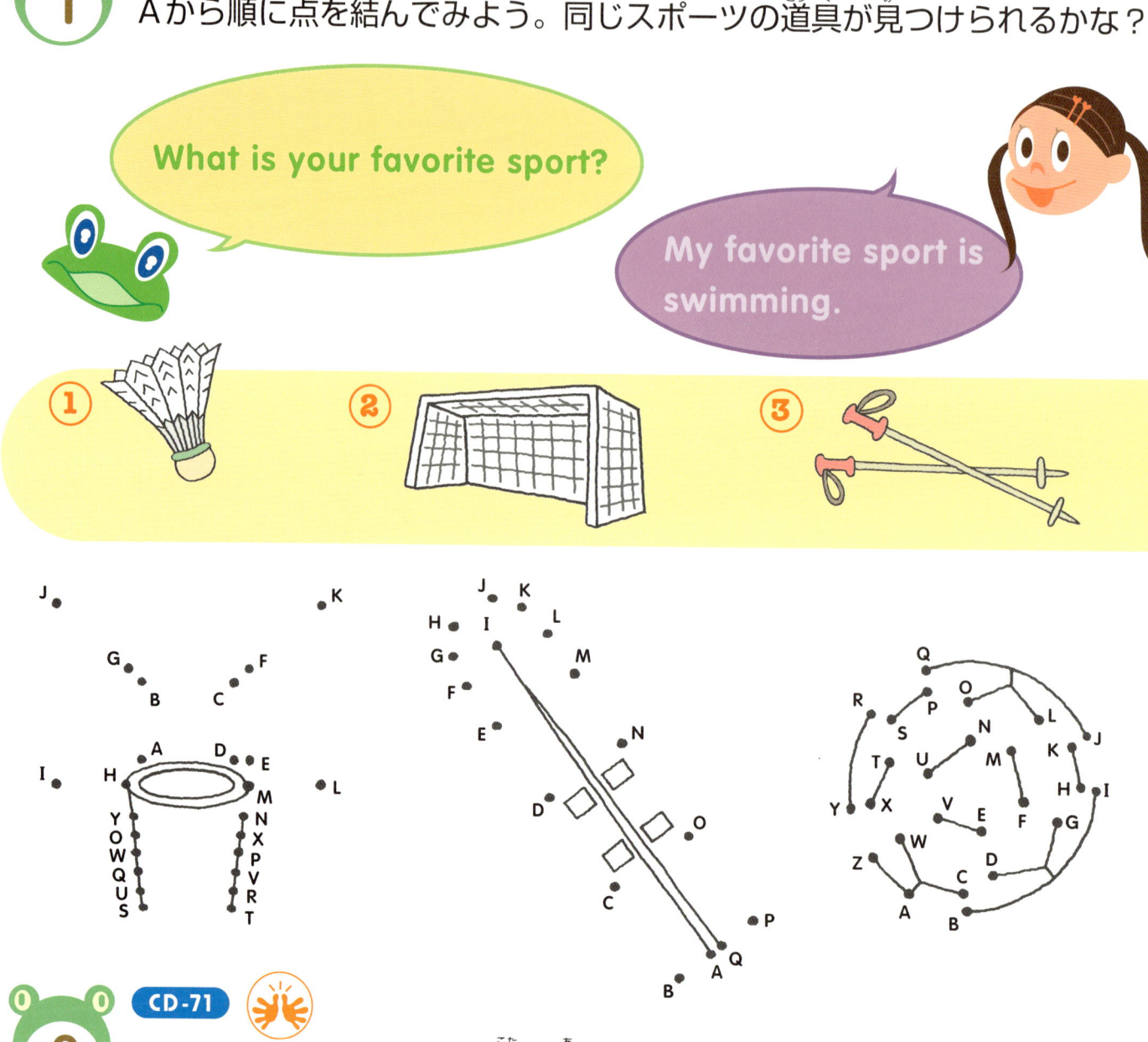

What is your favorite sport?

My favorite sport is swimming.

① ② ③

**2** CD-71 "Cheerleading Chant"で答え合わせをしよう。（答えは63ページ）

40 forty

スポーツにはいろいろな道具が使われているね。
どのスポーツにどんな道具が使われているか、知っているかな？

**CD-72**

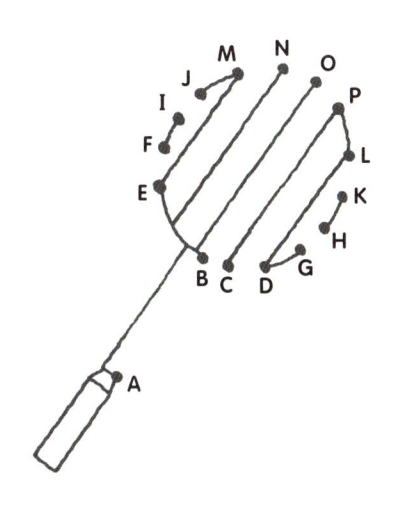

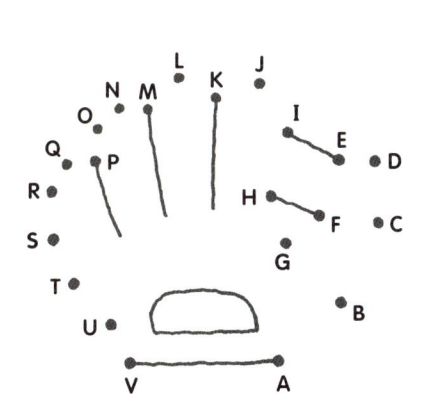

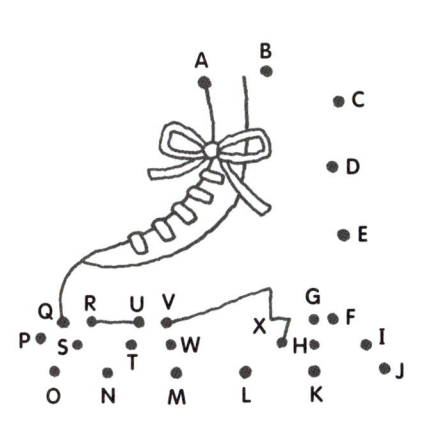

All About Me

あなたの好きなスポーツは何かな？
絵をかいて言ってみよう。

Me

④　⑤　⑥

forty-one

# Unit 19
# Rhyming House
## 家の中でライミング

**1** 　CD-73　　"On, In, Under Chant"に合わせて手を動かしながら言ってみよう。

on　　in　　under

**2** 　CD-74　CD-75　　"Rhyming Chant"を聞きながら、同じ音で終わる言葉を家の中から見つけてみよう。（答えは63ページ）

42　forty-two

耳をすまして、ぼくとミサの英語を
よく聞いてみてね。
おもしろい音のリズムに気づいたかな？

Where is the cat?

The cat is on the mat.

# Unit 20
# Follow Your Dream
## 大人になったら何になる？

**1** CD-76 会話を聞いて、それぞれの仕事の会話と絵のちがうところを見つけてね。

（答えは63ページ）

What do you want to be in the future?

① CD-77

② CD-78

③ CD-79

④ CD-80

ぼくたちのまわりにはいろいろな仕事をしている人がいるね。
みんなは大きくなったら何になりたい？

I want to be a vet.

**All About Me** CD-81

あなたが大きくなったらなりたいものをかいて言ってみよう。

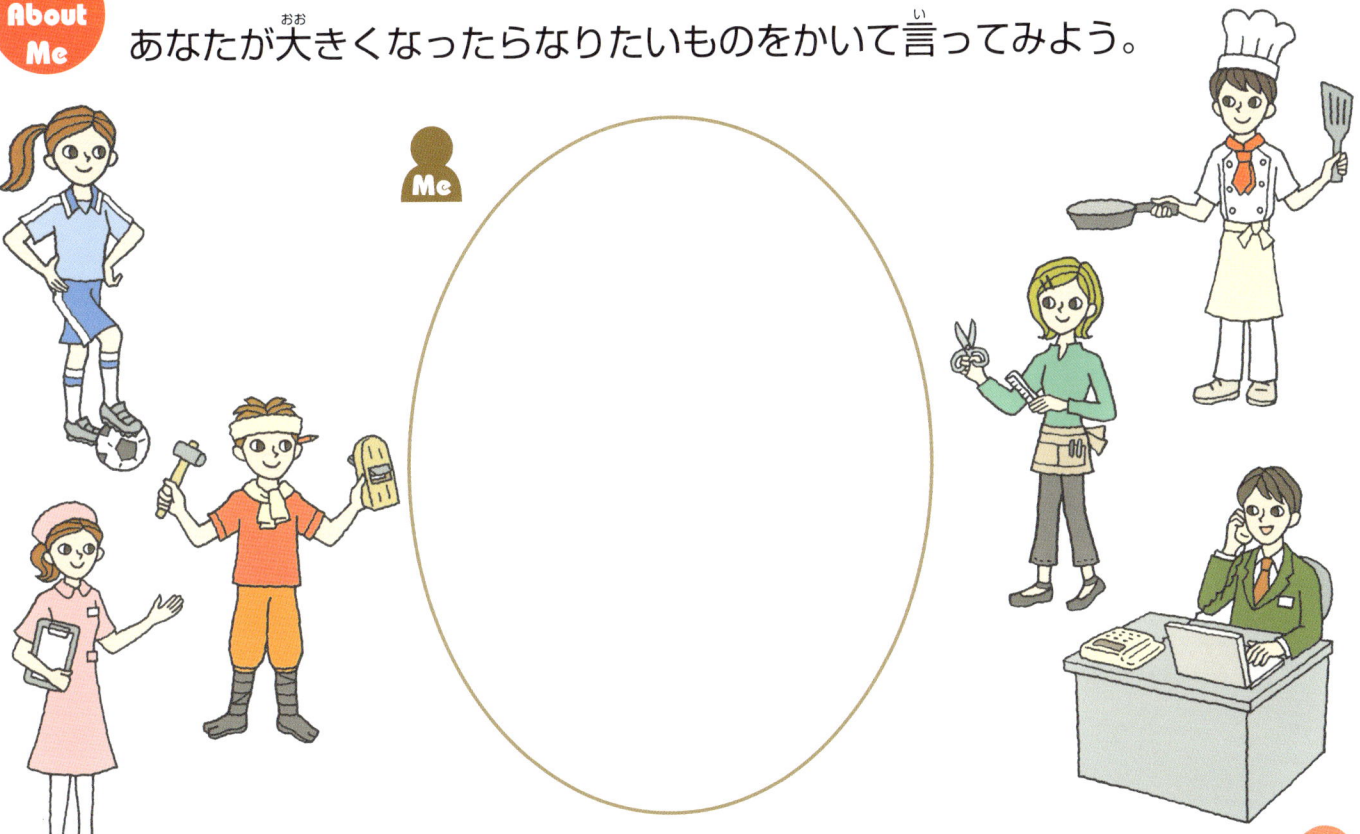

Me

# Unit 21
# Misa's One Fine Day
## ミサの一日

**1** CD-82

"Can You Chant"に合わせて、動物たちのまねをしてみよう。

What time do you get up?

**All About Me** あなたの一日の行動を英語で言ってみよう。

Me

みんなは毎日、なん時に起きる？
ミサとどっちが早起きかな？
みんなとミサの一日をくらべてみよう。

**2** CD-83 会話を聞いて、ミサの時計に時こくを入れてみよう。（答えは63ページ）

7:00

I get up at 7:00.

forty-seven 47

# Unit 22
# Storytelling
## カエルの王子様

**1** 🐸 CD-84 お話を聞いてみよう。

**2** 🐸 CD-85 もう一度聞いて、ぬけているセリフを言ってみよう。

ミサとぼくは学芸会でげきをしているよ。
どんなお話か、わかるかな？
物語をよく聞いてみてね。

**3**

**4**

**7**

**8**

Did you enjoy the games?

Yes, I had fun!

# ゲームの手引きとCDスクリプト

このページでは、おうちの方や先生方のためのゲームの手引きを各Unitごとに掲載しています。
また、付属のCDに収録されている音声の内容も合わせて掲載しましたので、お子さんといっしょに遊ぶ際の参考にしてください。

## このページの見方

**＜おうちの方、先生方へ＞**
おうちの方、先生方のためのゲームの手引きです。
数字は、それぞれのUnitの設問の番号に対応しています。

**＜スクリプト＞**
CDに収録されている音声の内容です。
Fはフロギーのセリフ、Mはミサのセリフをそれぞれ表しています。
また、太字は各Unitの中で特に重要な表現、赤い下線の部分は自分のことを言うのに使う表現です。

| | |
|---|---|
| **1.** | 設問の番号 |
| **CD-02** | CDのトラック番号 |
| 🎵 | 歌 |
| ✨ | チャンツ |

各Unitのタイトルの部分の色は、ゲームの取り組みやすさの目安を表しています。
ピンク→黄色→水色の順に、より英語に慣れ親しんだお子さん向けの内容になっていきます。

## Nice to Meet You! P.5
### はじめまして！

**＜おうちの方、先生方へ＞**
**1.** フロギー（Froggy）と小学校3年生のミサ（Misa）と一緒にゲームの始まりです。英語の音をたくさん聞き、声を出してゲームをしましょう。CDを聞きながら挨拶の練習をします。相手の目を見てはっきり挨拶することが大切です。**All About Me**では自信を持って自分の事を英語で言いましょう。

**＜スクリプト＞**
**1. CD-01**

F : Hi. I'm Froggy. What's your name?

M : Hello, Froggy. **My name is Misa**. Nice to meet you.

F : Nice to meet you, too. I'm soooo excited to play games with you. Why don't you write your name and draw your picture here? And every time you hear the sound, press the pause button and start the games. Now are you ready, Misa?

M : Yes! Let's get started!

## Unit 1 P.6~7
### Alphabet Jingle & Chant
### アルファベットでお口のたいそう

**＜おうちの方、先生方へ＞**
**1.** アルファベットの名前と音に慣れましょう。
**2.** ミサとフロギーのI Like Chantを聞いてみましょう。

**All About Me**：ジングル表にあるものの中から好きなものを選んでI Like Chantをリズム良く言いましょう。

**＜スクリプト＞**
**1. CD-02**

F : Misa, do you know how many letters there are in the alphabet?

M : 🎵 A, B, C, D, E, F, G, H, I, J, K, L, M, N, O, P, Q, R, S, T, U, V, W, X, Y, and Z. There are 26.

F : Right. How many *hiragana* letters do you have in Japanese?

M : We have about 50.

F : Exactly. And you have *kanji* and *katakana* letters as well. Now each alphabet letter has its own name and sound. Shall we start *The Alphabet Jingle*?

M : Yes, let's!

**CD-03**

F&M: A, a, a, a, apple; B, b, b, b, ball; C, c, c, c, cat; D, d, d, d, duck; E, e, e, e, egg; F, f, f, f, fish; G, g, g, g, green; H, h, h, h, horse; I, i, i, i, ink; J, j, j, j, jacket; K, k, k, k, kite; L, l, l, l, lion; M, m, m, m, monkey; N, n, n, n, noodle; O, o, o, o, octopus; P, p, p, p, pizza; Q, q, q, q, question; R, r, r, r, rain; S, s, s, s, sandwich; T, t, t, t, tomato; U, u, u, u, umbrella; V, v, v, v, violin; W, w, w, w, worm; X, x, x, x, box; Y, y, y, y, yo-yo; Z, z, z, z, zigzag.

**2. CD-04**

F: Excellent! Now let's chant the *I Like Chant*. Misa, which is your favorite picture card?

M: **H, Horse. H, H, Horse.** What about you, Froggy?

F: M, Monkey. M, M, Monkey.

**All About Me**

F: Now, it's your turn, everybody. Which picture card do you like best? Copy the first letter and chant!

## Unit 2
### Color Your Outfits
### 洋服はどんな色？
P.8〜9

＜おうちの方、先生方へ＞

**1.** What color〜の質問に答えて色をぬりましょう。（解答p.62）

**2.** *Mary is Wearing*を替え歌にして歌います。Maryのところを I（自分）に替えて歌いましょう。

**All About Me**: 自分の好きな洋服を入れて歌いましょう。

＜スクリプト＞

**1. CD-05**

F: Hi, everybody. I'm visiting Misa's room now. Hi, Misa! Ooops, what a mess! What are you doing, Misa?

M: Hi, Froggy. Come on in. Tomorrow is my grandfather's birthday so…

F: So you are choosing your dress for the party.

M: That's right.

F: Misa, I don't know why, but some of your clothes have no colors. What color is your hat?

M: It's red.

F: Okay, then what color is your sweater?

M: It's blue.

F: What about your pants and bag? What color are they?

M: Brown.

F: I see a shirt in your closet. What color is it?

M: My shirt is orange.

F: Now my last question. What color is your jacket?

M: Black.

F: Thanks for telling me, Misa. And what are you going to wear tomorrow?

M: This yellow dress, white socks and green shoes.

F: That should look great on you, Misa!

M: Thank you, Froggy.

**2. CD-06**

M: *Mary is Wearing*（替え歌）

I am wearing my yellow dress, yellow dress, yellow dress. I am wearing my yellow dress all day long.

**All About Me**

M: **I am wearing my yellow dress, white socks and green shoes.** What about you?

## Unit 3
### This is My Family
### ミサの家族しょうかい
P.10〜11

＜おうちの方、先生方へ＞

**1.** ミサの親戚がおじいさんの誕生祝に集まりました。ＣＤの会話を聞きながら、ミサの家族を当ててください。（解答p.62）

**All About Me**: 自分の家族を紹介しましょう。

＜スクリプト＞

**1. CD-07**

F: Misa, what is this?

M: This is my family picture. Yesterday was my grandfather's birthday party.

F: And these people are your family, and your uncle's and aunt's family, aren't they?

M: That's right. Fourteen people and three pets.

F: Who is this tall man wearing black pants?

M: That is my father. He likes cooking.

F: Who is this boy playing with a hamster?

M: That is my brother. He loves animals.

F: Who is this woman wearing a green dress?

M: That is my mother. She likes reading.

F: Is this your pet, too?

M: Yes. That is my pet, Choco. He is a cute brown dog.

**CD-08 All About Me**

M:**This is my grandfather. He is wearing a yellow shirt. He likes watching TV.** Tell us about your family.

## Unit 4      P.12〜13
## Who Says Oink, Oink?
### だれの鳴き声かな？

＜おうちの方、先生方へ＞

**1.**Old MacDonald Had a Farm を聞いて出てくる動物の順番にメイズを通ってゴールまで行きます。（CDの番号順で、解答p.62）

**2.**Cock-a-doodle-dooと鳴く動物はなんでしょう？数字をたどって点を結んでください。（解答p.62）

**All About Me**: 自分の飼っている動物、飼いたい動物の絵を描いて英語で言ってみましょう。

＜スクリプト＞

**1.CD-09**

F : Oh, Misa. Where are you going?

M: To my friend's farm.

F : Oh, you've got to walk the maze. Good luck, Misa!

M: Thanks, Froggy. I'll do my best.

**CD-10**

Old MacDonald Had a Farm

Old MacDonald had a farm, ee-igh, ee-igh, oh!

And on this farm he had some chicks, ee-igh, ee-igh, oh!

With a chick, chick here, and a chick, chick there.

Here a chick, there a chick, everywhere a chick, chick.

Old MacDonald had a farm, ee-igh, ee-igh, oh!

（2番以降、動物の名前と鳴き声を入れ替えて歌う。）

ducks - quack; turkeys - gobble; pigs - oink

**2.CD-11**

F : Now, everybody, this is a guessing game. What animal says cock-a-doodle-doo? Connect the numbers from 1 to 30. What do you see?

**CD-12   All About Me**

F : Misa, do you have any pets?

M:**Yes, I have a dog. My dog's name is Choco.** Do you have any pets, everybody? Do you have a cat, a bird, a hamster or a turtle? Tell me about your pet or a pet you want.

## Unit 5      P.14〜15
## Fruits & Vegetables
### くだものと野菜さがし

＜おうちの方、先生方へ＞

**1.**果樹園には果物、畑には野菜が隠れています。どこにあるか探してみましょう。（CDの番号順で、解答p.62）

**All About Me**: 自分の好きな果物、野菜のチャンツを作って歌いましょう。

＜スクリプト＞

**1.CD-13**

F : I see lots of fruits and vegetables.

M: Yes. The fruits look yummy.

F : Where are the apples?

M: They are on the tree.

F : Okay, everybody. Can you find eight kinds of fruits and eight kinds of vegetables in the picture?

**CD-14**

F : Now it's time to check your answers.

Fruit & Vegetable Chant

Apples, peaches, cherries and oranges. These are the fruits that grow on trees. Watermelons, pineapples, strawberries and melons. These are the fruits that grow on land. Tomatoes, cucumbers, eggplants and corn. These are the vegetables that grow on land. Carrots, potatoes, onions and daikons. These are the vegetables that grow under ground.

**CD-15   All About Me**

M: Apples, peaches, eggplants and corn. These are the things I like to eat. **I like apples, peaches, eggplants and corn.** What fruits and vegetables do you like?

## Unit 6　P.16〜17
### Numbers & Shapes Maze
### 数字と形のめいろへようこそ

**＜おうちの方、先生方へ＞**

**1.** 三角形をたどってゴールへ。途中4ヶ所の宝箱でCDを聞いて計算問題を解きます。その後、計算問題の答えをCDで聞き取ってください。（CDの番号順で、解答p.62）

**2.** *Twinkle, Twinkle, Little Star* を歌いながら、三角形以外の形も探してください。（解答p.62）

**All About Me**：自分に関係のある数字を英語で言います。

**＜スクリプト＞**

**1. CD-16**

F：Misa is in the maze. Do you see many different shapes in the maze? Misa has to walk through only on triangles. Can you help her?

M：Please help me, everybody.

F：When you come to each treasure box, don't forget to listen to the CD. Answer the questions and write the numbers in the boxes.

**CD-17**

Q1：One plus three equals….

Q2：Two plus five equals….

Q3：Six minus two equals….

Q4：Eight minus four equals…..

**CD-18**

F：Has Misa reached the goal? Good. Now let's check your answers.

Q1：One plus three equals four.

Q2：Two plus five equals seven.

Q3：Six minus two equals four.

Q4：Eight minus four equals four.

**2. CD-19**

F：Now let's look for other shapes. How many squares, stars and circles are there? Sing *Twinkle, Twinkle, Little Star* and count the shapes.

*Twinkle, Twinkle, Little Star*

Twinkle, twinkle, little star, how I wonder what you are. Up above the world so high, like a diamond in the sky. Twinkle, twinkle, little star, how I wonder what you are.

**CD-20　All About Me**

M：**I'm eight years old. My phone number is 123-0987. I have three erasers.** Now it's your turn. How old are you? What's your phone number? How many erasers do you have?

## Unit 7　P.18〜19
### Jump Rope Rhymes
### なわとび歌で遊ぼう

**＜おうちの方、先生方へ＞**

**1.** 実際に縄跳びをしながら歌いましょう。

**All About Me**：自分ができることを言ってみましょう。

**＜スクリプト＞**

**1. CD-21**

F：Misa, can you jump rope?

M：Yes, I can.

F：How many times can you jump without missing?

M：I can jump more than 26 times. Look, Froggy.

*Alphabet Soup*

A, B, C in the alphabet soup. What will I find in the alphabet soup? A, B, C, D, E, F, G…Z.

F：Wow, that's cool, Misa. Now what about you, everybody? Try all the jump rope rhymes!

**CD-22**

*I Love Coffee*

I love coffee, I love tea. I love the boys, and the boys love me!

**CD-23**

*Teddy Bear*

Teddy bear, teddy bear, turn around.（下線部を繰り返す）Touch the ground. Show your shoe. That will do. Go upstairs. Say your prayers. Turn off the light. Say goodnight.

**CD-24　All About Me**

F：Misa, can you jump rope? Can you roller skate? Can you whistle? Can you touch your nose with your tongue? Can you say the alphabet from A to Z?

M：**Yes, I can jump rope. I can roller skate. I can whistle. I can say the alphabet from A to Z.** Now, what can you do?

fifty-three

## Unit 8    P.20〜21
### Toys Spot the Difference
### クリスマスまちがいさがし

<おうちの方、先生方へ>

**1.** イラストの間違いを6ヶ所見つけます。*Jingle Bells*を歌いながら探しましょう。

**2.** ＣＤの会話を聞きながら答え合わせをします。（CDの番号順で、解答p.62）

<スクリプト>

**1. CD-25**

F : Let's play the *Spot the Difference Game*. Here we have two pictures of Christmas Eve. Can you find six different things in the two pictures?

M : Well. Let's see… Oh, I found one.

F : Now, everybody, try to spot six differences with Misa.

**CD-26**

🎵 *Jingle Bells*

Dashing through the snow in a one-horse open sleigh,
O'er the fields we go, Laughing all the way;

Bells on bob-tail ring, making spirits bright,

What fun it is to ride and sing a sleighing song tonight.

Jingle bells, jingle bells, jingle all the way!

Oh, what fun it is to ride, in a one-horse open sleigh.
（繰り返し）

**2. CD-27**

F : Time's up. Let's check the answers together.
What did you find first?

M : The presents.     …①

F : Bingo. How many presents are there in Picture A?

M : Ten.

F : But in Picture B there are eleven. Okay and next?

M : The Christmas tree.     …②

F : You are right. In Picture A the Christmas tree is…

M : Short.

F : But in Picture B…

M : The Christmas tree is tall.

F : Exactly. You are right. And on the Christmas tree, something is wrong.

M : Yes, Santa Claus and an angel. …③

F : And the colors are different as well. In Picture A one of the stockings is…     …④

M : Red and green.

F : But in Picture B…

M : Pink and green.

F : Great, Misa. Now what about something on the sofa?

M : A cat is on the sofa.     …⑤

F : And in Picture A…

M : A cat is sleeping.

F : And in Picture B…

M : A cat is yawning.

F : Awesome! Now one more to go!

M : A gingerbread house on the table.

F : Yes. What is in the house?     …⑥

M : In Picture A, a gingerbread man is in the house.

F : But in Picture B…

M : Froggy is in the house.

F : Super dee duper! You could spot all the differences, Misa. Congratulations!

## Unit 9    P.22〜23
### Shopping List Code
### 買い物に行こう

<おうちの方、先生方へ>

**1.** 買い物リストの絵を見て、ミサが買う物を書きましょう。

**2.** 買い物の歌を聞いて答え合わせをします。（解答p.62）

**3.** 地図に買い物をする道順をかき込んでください。（解答p.62）

**All About Me** : 自分の町の店とそこで買う物の歌を歌います。

<スクリプト>

**1. CD-28**

F : Where are you going, Misa?

M : 🎵 I'm going to the store. （繰り返し） I'm going to the bookstore to buy a book. I'm going to the bookstore to buy a book.

F : You know what? 🎵 I'm going to the store. （繰り返し） I'm going to the grocery store to buy some fruits. I'm going to the grocery store to buy some fruits.

M : That's good. Let's go shopping together.

F : What's that in your hand, Misa?

M : This is a shopping list.

F : Oh, Misa, you have to read these secret codes. Let me see. Um, I got it. Everybody, do you know what Misa is supposed to buy? Read the codes for her.

**2. CD-29**

F: ① An apple. Misa went to the grocery store to buy an apple.

② Four eggs. Misa went to the supermarket to buy four eggs.

③ A loaf of bread. Misa went to the bakery to buy a loaf of bread.

④ Three pencils. Misa went to the stationery store to buy three pencils.

⑤ A yo-yo. Misa went to the toy shop to buy a yo-yo.

⑥ A book. Misa went to the bookstore to buy a book.

**3.** F: Now, everybody, draw Misa's shopping route on the map.

**CD-30　All About Me**

M: I'm going to the store. （繰り返し） **I'm going to the bookstore to buy a book.** What about you?

## Unit 10　　P.24〜25
### Sing & Draw Vehicles
### のりもの絵かき歌

＜おうちの方、先生方へ＞

**1.** CDの絵描き歌を聞いて乗り物を当てます。4コマ目に続きをかいて乗り物の絵を完成させましょう。

**All About Me**: オリジナルの海の乗り物を描きましょう。

＜スクリプト＞

**1. CD-31**

F: Let's doodle, everybody. I'm going to sing and draw three vehicles. Trace the lines and sing together. Draw the complete pictures in the last boxes.

**CD-32**

The Wheels on the Bus（替え歌）

F&M: **First draw one circle, round and round,** （3回繰り返し）. **Next draw another circle, round and round. And one long, long snake.**

F: What's this?

M: It's a car!

**CD-33**

F&M: **First draw one triangle, one, two, three,** （3回繰り返し）. Next draw another triangle, one, two, three. And two circles in the front and back.

F: What's this?

M: It's a bike!

**CD-34**

F&M: First draw one line from left to right, （3回繰り返し）. Next put one oval on the line. And a half circle at the end.

F: What's this?

M: It's a helicopter!

**CD-35　All About Me**

M: Now it's your turn! Use circles, triangles, squares, rectangles, ovals, lines and other shapes and draw a vehicle on the sea.

## Unit 11　　P.26〜27
### Origami Newspaper
### 新聞で折り紙をしよう

＜おうちの方、先生方へ＞

**1.** アメリカにも日本と同様に新聞紙でつくる帽子があります。CDを聞きながらかぶとと帽子を作りましょう。（CDの番号順で）

**2.** 実際に作ってマジックの答えを当てます。（解答p.62）

＜スクリプト＞

**1. CD-36**

F: Misa, do you know how to make a hat from newspaper?

M: Yes. I can make *kabuto*.

F: Good. Here I have a sheet of newspaper. How do you make *kabuto*?

M: ① First, fold the newspaper and make a triangle.

② Then, cut off **A** and unfold.

③ Fold the square paper into a triangle.

④ Fold two corners down.

⑤ Fold up the two points.

⑥ Fold two corners **B** and fold one sheet up along the line.

⑦ Fold **C** again and tuck another sheet **D** inside. Kabuto is done.

**CD-37**

F: Spectacular, Misa! Now it's my turn.

① First, fold the newspaper in half.

② Then, fold the two points inside.

③ Fold up twice. Flip it and fold up twice again.

④ Put strips of paper on top of the hat.

M: Froggy, I like your hat. It's cute.

**2. CD-38**

F : And now boys and girls, it's magic show time. First, cut a long piece of paper. Next, give it a half twist. Then, paste the ends together. Finally, cut along the center of the band. What do you think will happen?

## Unit 12    P.28〜29
### The School Sugoroku
### 学校すごろくで遊ぼう

<おうちの方、先生方へ>
**1.** 学校すごろくで遊びましょう。さいころを用意して出た数だけ進み、教科のコマにきたらCDを聞きます。問題がある箇所は答えてください。（CDの番号順で、解答p.62）

**All About Me**: 自分の好きな科目を言いましょう。

<スクリプト>

**1. CD-39**

F : Good morning, Misa. Are you going to school now? Have a nice day.

M : Good morning, Froggy. See you later.

F : Now, everybody, let's start *Misa's School Sugoroku*.

**CD-40**

Every morning at eight o'clock, Misa gets started her day at school. Her very first class is Japanese. Q1:How do you say "school" in Japanese?

**CD-41**

Her second period is mathematics. Plus, minus, times and divided by. Q2:Five frogs and two chickens. How many legs in all?

**CD-42**

Arts and crafts. Arts and crafts. Misa likes painting in arts and crafts.

**CD-43**

This is the very last class before lunch. She's good at experiments in science class.

**CD-44**

Her favorite subject English is after lunch. Misa loves singing lots of English songs. Q3:Say this; Red lemon. Yellow lemon. （2回繰り返す）

**CD-45**

Organ, drum, recorder, and castanet. She loves to play the instruments in music class. Q4:Sing *The ABC Song* from Z to A. Z, Y, X, W, V, U, T...

**CD-46**

Swim, run, jump and throw and kick. These are the actions she does in PE. Q5:Hop ten times with your eyes closed.

**CD-47**

History and geography. Misa likes to learn about Japan and the world.

F : Awesome, everybody! Now Misa is coming back home!

**CD-48  All About Me**

M : I'm home, Froggy. How was the *School Sugoroku*? Now, everybody, **my favorite subject is English**. What's your favorite subject?

## Unit 13    P.30〜31
### Vacation Mix-Up
### 海や山で何して遊ぶ？

<おうちの方、先生方へ>
**1.** 山や海で楽しそうに人々が遊んでいます。おかしなところを探してCDで答えあわせをしましょう。（CDの番号順で、解答p.63）

<スクリプト>

**1. CD-49**

F : Misa, where are you going this summer?

M : I'm going to the beach. I love swimming.

F : That sounds exciting. I'm planning to go to the mountains.

M : Have fun!

F : Thanks. Look, Misa. I have pictures of summer and winter vacation. But, uh-oh, something is wrong. Can you spot the differences? What's wrong, Misa?

**CD-50**

M : Oh, my goodness.

① A boy is snowboarding.
② A polar bear is on the beach.
③ An old man is in a ski suit.
④ A man is skating on the water.
⑤ Children are throwing snow balls.
⑥ A mountain climber is climbing the rocks.
⑦ Skiers are sitting around the fire.
⑧ A tree with red autumn leaves stands on the beach.

**CD-51**

F : Oh, no.
  ① A girl is wearing a swimsuit.
  ② A lifeguard is sitting in a tall chair.
  ③ A beach umbrella is on the ski slope.
  ④ A boy is water skiing.
  ⑤ Girls are playing in the pool.
  ⑥ A woman is sleeping on an air mattress.
  ⑦ A man is climbing with sandals.
  ⑧ One tropical fish is swimming under the ice.

## Unit 14　Friends & Feelings　p.32〜33
気持ちをあらわす言葉

〈おうちの方、先生方へ〉

**1.** *Let's Make a Face*を歌いましょう。happy, sadの他に、tired, surprisedなどいろいろな表情を作ってみましょう。（CDの番号順で）

**2.** CDを聞いて、色々な気持ちの表現を練習しましょう。

**3.** フロギーはアメリカで使われているsmiley、ミサは日本の顔文字を使って、どんな時にどんな気持ちになるかを絵文字で書いています。読み解いてください。（解答p.63）

**All About Me**：どんな時楽しく、どんな時悲しいか絵をかいて英語で言ってみましょう。

〈スクリプト〉

**1. CD-52**

F : Misa, do you know this?　Let's make a face, a happy, happy face. Eyes, ears, mouth and nose. Happy!

M : Yeah, I know that, Froggy.　Let's make a face, a sad, sad face. Eyes, ears, mouth and nose. Sad!

F : What about this one?　Let's make a face, a funny, funny face. Eyes, ears, mouth and nose. Funny!

M : Yuck. Your face is soooo funny.

**2. CD-53**

F : Misa, how do you feel now? Are you happy?

M : Yes, I'm happy.

F : Everybody, what about you? How do you feel now? Let's practice nine expressions. I'm angry. I'm surprised. I'm tired. I'm sleepy. I'm bored. I'm hungry. I'm thirsty. I'm hot. I'm cold.

**3. CD-54**

F : There are different kinds of face marks in the world. Can you read my American smileys and Misa's Japanese smileys? Try reading them!

F : Were you able to decode our messages? Now the answers are...

F : I'm happy when I can jump high. I'm sad when I oversleep. I'm angry when I'm lied to.

M : **I'm happy when I eat ice cream.** I'm sad when I get bad scores. I'm angry when I'm teased.

**CD-55  All About Me**

F : Now it's your turn. When are you happy? When do you become sad? When do you get angry?

## Unit 15　Homes of Wild Animals　p.34〜35
動物たちのふるさと

〈おうちの方、先生方へ〉

**1.** 動物園にいる動物にはそれぞれ故郷があります。世界地図をよく見て国々の気候や地形を学びます。（CDの番号順で）

CDを聞きながら1-6番の動物をあてます。（解答p.63）

**All About Me**：自分の好きな動物を選んで3つのヒントを考え、友達に問題を出してみましょう。

〈スクリプト〉

**1. CD-56**

F : Here we are at the zoo. Misa, what animal do you like best?

M : I like zebras because they are beautiful. What animal do you like best?

F : I like giraffes because they are very tall. By the way, Misa, every animal in the zoo has its own home country. Where are koalas from?

M : They are from Australia.

**CD-57**

F : You got it. Now shall we play the *Three-Hint Game*? Listen to the hints and guess the animals.

① **This animal has a long nose. Its ears are big. It is from Africa, Area A. What is it?**

**CD-58**

② This animal is black and yellow. It is an endangered animal. It is from Southeast Asia, Area D. What is it?

**CD-59**

③ This animal has a big mouth with teeth. It is very dangerous. It is from North America, Area F. What is it?

**CD-60**

④ This animal is black and white. It eats bamboo. It is from China, Area C. What is it?

**CD-61**

⑤ This animal has white fur. It is very big. It is from the North Pole, Area B. What is it?

**CD-62**

⑥ This animal has a long tail. It can jump very well. It is from Australia, Area E. What is it?

**CD-63** **All About Me**

M: Now it's your turn to make your own *Three-Hint Game*. Choose one animal from the map.（Asia）crane, monkey, panda, tiger, elephant, camel,（Australia）koala, kangaroo,（Europe）wolf, fox, moose,（Africa）hippopotamus, elephant, zebra, giraffe, lion,（North America）bear, snake, alligator,（South America）snake, jaguar,（Antarctica）penguin, seal,（the North Pole）polar bear.

## Unit 16  P.36〜37
### Cooking Bingo
### 今日のごはんは何かな？

＜おうちの方、先生方へ＞

**1.** まず右のビンゴを使ってミサと対戦しましょう。次にカバーにある料理の絵を切り取って自分のオリジナルのビンゴを作り、再びミサと対戦してください。（CDの番号順で）

**All About Me**: 自分の朝昼晩食べたい食事の絵を描いて、英語で言ってみましょう。

＜スクリプト＞

**1. CD-64**

F: Misa, would you like to play *Cooking Bingo*?

M: Sure. Can I choose the left card, everybody?

F: Okey-dokey. Then the rest of you choose the right one.
　Are you ready? Now let's get started.

🌞 Food Chant

（2回ずつ繰り返す）Toast, bacon and eggs, fruits, rice, natto, sandwich, miso soup, hamburger, pizza, ramen, hotdog, French fries, salad, spaghetti, steak...

M: I got Bingo!

F: You did it, Misa! Shall we go on? Curry and rice....Bingo? Oh, you got bingo, too? Good. Now, everybody, this time you can make your own bingo. Cut out twenty four dishes from the cover of this book and place them on the card below. When you're ready, I'm gonna start calling!

**CD-65**

F: 🌞（2回ずつ繰り返す）Bacon and eggs, croquette, curry and rice, fish, French fries, fried prawn, fruits, hamburger, hamburger steak, hotdog, juice, milk, miso soup, natto, pizza, ramen, rice, salad, sandwich, soup, spaghetti, steak, tea, toast.

**CD-66** **All About Me**

F: How was Bingo, everybody? Now let's talk about what you like to eat for breakfast, lunch and dinner. Now, Misa, <u>what do you like to eat for breakfast?</u>

M: <u>I like to eat toast</u> **for breakfast, curry and rice for lunch, and spaghetti for dinner.** What about you?

## Unit 17  P.38〜39
### Misa's Garden Story
### 庭で野菜ができるまで

＜おうちの方、先生方へ＞

**1.** フロギーがミサのお庭物語を作ってくれました。ミサの朗読を聞きましょう。（CDの番号順で）

**2.** *Story Chant*を聞きながら、バラバラに並んだイラストを物語の順番に戻して声に出して言ってみましょう。（解答p.63）

＜スクリプト＞

**1. CD-67**

F: 🎵 *Oats, Peas, Beans, & Barley Grow*

<u>Oats, peas, beans, and barley grow.</u>（繰り返し）Do you or I or anyone know how oats, peas, beans, and barley grow?

M: <u>What are you doing, Froggy?</u>  What song is this?

F: It's a song about growing plants. Misa, I made *Misa's Garden Story*. Would you read the story to everybody?

M: Yes, I'd love to.

**CD-68**

M: This is my garden. I am raking the soil. I am planting the seeds. <u>I am watering the seeds.</u> I am pulling the weeds. The sun is shining. I am picking the tomatoes.

**2. CD-69**

F : Now, everybody, put the cards in the order of the story and chant! ✸（2回ずつ繰り返す）Rake the soil. Plant the seeds. Water the seeds. Pull the weeds. The sun is shining. Pick the tomatoes. That's it!

## Unit 18     P.40〜41
## Sports Dot-to-Dot
### スポーツ大好き

<おうちの方、先生方へ>
1. 点線を結んでスポーツに使われる道具を当てます。(CDの番号順で、解答p.63)
2. Cheerleading Chantを聴きながら答えあわせをします。

**All About Me**：自分の好きなスポーツを言ってみましょう。

<スクリプト>
**1. CD-70**

F : What is your favorite sport?

M : **My favorite sport is swimming.** What about you?

F : I like playing baseball. We use balls, bats and gloves. Now, Misa, you'll see the things used in six sports. Connect the dots and figure them out.

**2. CD-71**

M : Now let's check your answers along with the *Cheerleading Chant*.

✸ ① B-A-D-M-I-N-T-O-N. Shuttlecock, racket. I like playing badminton.

✸ ② S-O-C-C-E-R. Soccer goal, ball. Score a goal in the soccer game.

✸ ③ S-K-I-I-N-G. Poles, skis. Skiing is the best sport in winter.

✸ ④ B-A-S-K-E-T-B-A-L-L. Basketball, hoop. Basketball players are really cool.

✸ ⑤ S-K-A-T-I-N-G. Skating rink, skate. Figure skating, speed skating, ice hockey.

✸ ⑥ B-A-S-E-B-A-L-L. Bat, glove. Take me out to the baseball game.

**CD-72  All About Me**

F : Good job. Now tell me about yourself. What is your favorite sport?

## Unit 19     P.42〜43
## Rhyming House
### 家の中でライミング

<おうちの方、先生方へ>
1. 手を使ってon, in, underの位置を確認し、チャンツで場所を表すフレーズに慣れます。(CDの番号順で)
2. 同じ韻を踏む（ライミング）単語を見つけます。(解答p.63)

<スクリプト>
**1. CD-73**

F : ✸On the, in the, under the.（繰り返し）

M : What are you doing, Froggy?

F : ✸ On the, in the, under the. Misa, I see lots of things in your house. Listen to the *On, In, Under Chant*.

✸On the, in the, under the. Where is the cat?

M : The cat is on the mat.

F : ✸On the, in the, under the. Where is the duck?

M : The duck is in the truck.

F : ✸ On the, in the, under the. Where is the pan?

M : The pan is under the fan.

F : Terrific. Now, everybody, it's your turn. ✸On the, in the, under the. Where is the moon?

M : The moon is on the spoon.

F : Fantastic. ✸On the, in the, under the. Where are the socks?

M : The socks are in the box.

F : Way to go! ✸On the, in the, under the. Where is the bee?

M : The bee is under the tree.

**2. CD-74**

F : We can play another game, Misa.

M : What's next?

F : The Rhyming Game! Misa, can you find rhyming words?

M : Fat, cat..... hat..... and mat!

F : Fat, cat, hat, mat. A fat cat and a hat are on the mat. What else can you find?

fifty-nine

### CD-75

F : Now let's check with the *Rhyming Chant*.

① (hall and the front door) Coat, boat, goat. The boat and the goat are on the coat.

② (living room) Chair, bear, chair, bear: The bear is on the chair.

③ (kitchen) Dish, fish, dish, fish. The fish is on the dish.

④ (bedroom) Box, socks, box, socks. The socks are in the box.

⑤ (bathroom) Tub, cub, tub, cub. The cub is in the tub.

⑥ (garage) Duck, truck, duck, truck. The duck is on the truck.

⑦ (front yard) Mole, hole, mole, hole. The mole came out of the hole.

⑧ (backyard) Eight, skate, gate. Eight skates are on the gate.

## Unit 20  P.44～45
## Follow Your Dream
### 大人になったら何になる？

<おうちの方、先生方へ>

**1.** 職業に関する4枚の絵には間違いが1つずつあります。CDをよく聞いて見つけてください。会話を声に出して言ってみましょう。（CDの番号順で、解答p.63）

**All About Me**: 将来なりたい職業を言いましょう。

<スクリプト>

**1. CD-76**

F : Misa, what do you want to be in the future?

M : Well, I want to be a vet.

F : Misa, I'm sure your dream will come true. Now look at the pictures. You'll see four different jobs: a TV reporter, a flight attendant, a teacher, and a florist. Listen to the CD, look at the pictures carefully and find out one mistake in each picture. Are you ready?

### CD-77

①**TV reporter** T (TV reporter): "Good morning. It's a wonderful sunny morning. The spring flowers are beautiful out here in Central Park. We're expecting no rain today. Cooler than normal temperatures with a high of 62. In Central Park, Linda Brown, NY11."

### CD-78

②**Flight attendant** F (Flight attendant): "What would you like for dinner? We have chicken, fish and pasta tonight." P (Passenger): "I'll take fish." F: "Here you are. Enjoy your meal." P: "Thank you."

### CD-79

③**Teacher** T (Teacher): "Open your textbooks to page 20. Listen to this question. *There are ten dinosaurs and two whales and one mammoth in the museum. How many dinosaurs and mammoths are there in the museum?* Those who know the answer, raise your hands." S (Student): "Yes, Mr. Ishida." T: "Aki, come to the board and write the answer." T: "Well done, Aki."

### CD-80

④**Florist** F (Florist): "How may I help you?" C (Customer): "I'd like to have a flower bouquet arranged for my wife." F: "What kind of flowers does she like?" C: "She loves roses." F: "Okay, I'll make a bouquet with one dozen fresh-cut red roses and add some greenery." C: "That sounds lovely." F: "Here you are." C: "Thank you."

### CD-81 All About Me

M : **I want to be a vet. I want to help animals.** What about you? Do you want to be an athlete, a cook, a carpenter, a hairdresser, a nurse or an office worker? Tell us about your dream.

## Unit 21  P.46～47
## Misa's One Fine Day
### ミサの一日

<おうちの方、先生方へ>

**1.** *Can You Chant*を言いながら、色々な動作をしてみましょう。動物になったつもりでチャンツを言います。

**2.** ミサの一日をCDで聞いてみましょう。時計に数字を書き込んでください。（解答p.63）

**All About Me**: 自分の一日の行動の時間を書き込み、英語で言ってみましょう。

<スクリプト>

**1. CD-82**

F : Now let's do *Can You Chant*. Pretend that you are an animal. Can you fly, fly like a bird?

M : Can you walk, walk like an elephant?

F : Can you run, run like a squirrel?

M : Can you eat, eat like a lion?

F: Can you sleep, sleep like a bear?

M: Can you climb, climb like a monkey?

F: Can you laugh, laugh like a kookaburra?

M: Can you drink, drink like a horse?

F: Can you swim, swim like a seal?

M: Can you cry, cry like a baby?

**2. CD-83**

F: Let's ask Misa how she spends her day. Listen to the CD and fill in the missing time.

(In the morning) Misa, what time do you get up?

M: **I get up at seven.** Mom wakes me up.

F: Okay and what time do you have breakfast?

M: I have breakfast at seven-thirty. I usually eat cereal.

F: Then what time do you go to school?

M: I go to school at eight. I walk to school with my friend.

(In the afternoon)

F: Misa, what time do you have lunch?

M: I have lunch at twelve. Lunch time is my favorite.

F: What time do you come home from school?

M: I come home at three thirty. "Hi, Mom. I'm home."

F: Then what time do you play with your friends?

M: I play with my friends at four. We like to play cards.

(In the evening)

F: Misa, what time do you have dinner?

M: I have dinner at seven twenty. I always set the table.

F: And what time do you do your homework?

M: I do my homework at eight. Today's homework is art.

F: What time do you brush your teeth?

M: I brush my teeth at eight fifty. I do it with my brother.

F: What time do you go to bed?

M: I go to bed at nine. "Good night."

F: "Sleep tight."

**All About Me**

M: Now, everybody, it's your turn to tell us about your day.

## Unit 22
## Storytelling
### カエルの王子様

P.48〜49

＜おうちの方、先生方へ＞

**1.** 物語の朗読を聴きます。イラストをヒントに物語の内容を理解します。

**2.** 次にＣＤをもう一度聞いて抜けているセリフ（青色）の英語を言います。

**3.** 英語のゲームはいかがでしたか。何度も繰り返しフロギーとミサとゲームをしてくださいね。

＜スクリプト＞
**1.2. CD-84/85**

① Once upon a time, there was a lovely princess. She said, "I love this golden ball." She played by the well in the forest. ② One day when the princess was playing with the golden ball, she said, "Oh, I dropped the ball." ③ "Ribbit. Ribbit" a frog came out of the well with the golden ball and said. "Here you are." ④ The princess said, "Thank you." Then the frog said "Take me with you!" ⑤ The princess said, "Okay, come with me." Then the frog said, "Thank you, Princess." ⑥ The frog said, "I want to eat dinner with you." He also said, "I want to sleep in your bed." ⑦ The princess got angry and said, "I don't like you." She lifted the frog and threw him against the wall. ⑧ Then, suddenly, the frog turned into a young prince. The prince said, "Thank you for helping me." The prince and the princess lived happily ever after. The End.

**3. CD-86**

F: Did you enjoy the games?

M: Yes, I had fun! What about you, everybody?

F & M: We hope to see you soon! Enjoy English!

# 答えのページ

## Unit 2 (8ページ)

## Unit 3 (10〜11ページ)
father, mother, pet, brother

## Unit 4 (12ページ)

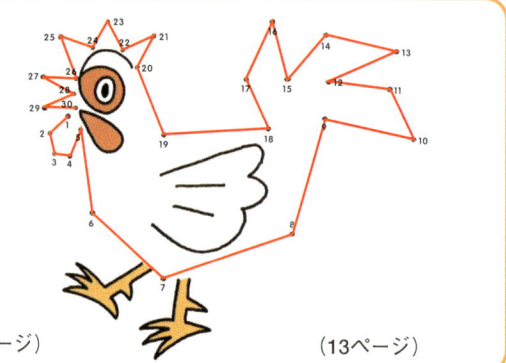

## (13ページ)

## Unit 5 (14ページ)

## Unit 6
(16ページ) 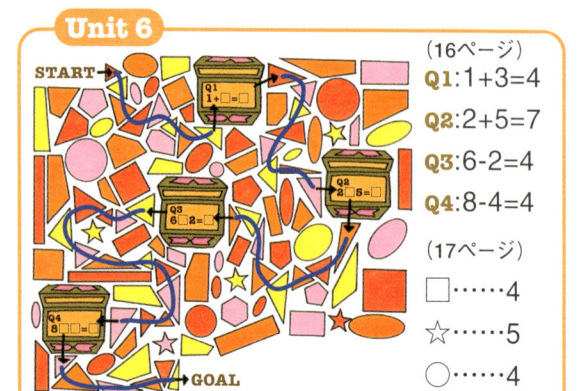
Q1: 1+3=4
Q2: 2+5=7
Q3: 6-2=4
Q4: 8-4=4

(17ページ)
□……4
☆……5
○……4

## Unit 8 (20〜21ページ)

## Unit 9
(22ページ)
1 りんご (an apple)
2 たまご (four eggs)
3 パン (a loaf of bread)
4 えんぴつ (three pencils)
5 ヨーヨー (a yo-yo)
6 本 (a book)

(23ページ)

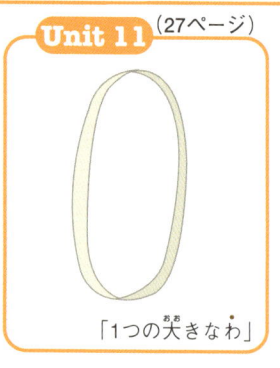

## Unit 11 (27ページ)
「1つの大きなわ」

## Unit 12 (28〜29ページ)
(Japanese) 学校
(Math) 24

## Unit 13 (30～31ページ)

## Unit 14 (33ページ)

**Froggy**

I'm happy when I can jump high.
I'm sad when I oversleep.
I'm angry when I'm lied to.

**Misa**

I'm happy when I eat ice cream.
I'm sad when I get bad scores.
I'm angry when I'm teased.

## Unit 15 (34～35ページ)

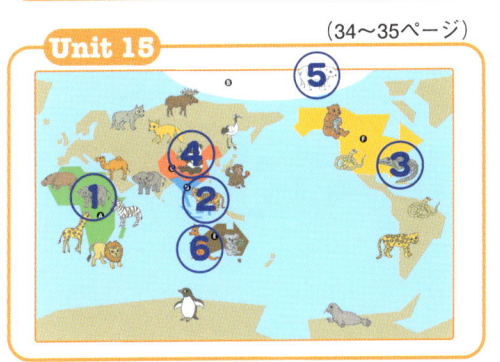

## Unit 18 (40～41ページ)

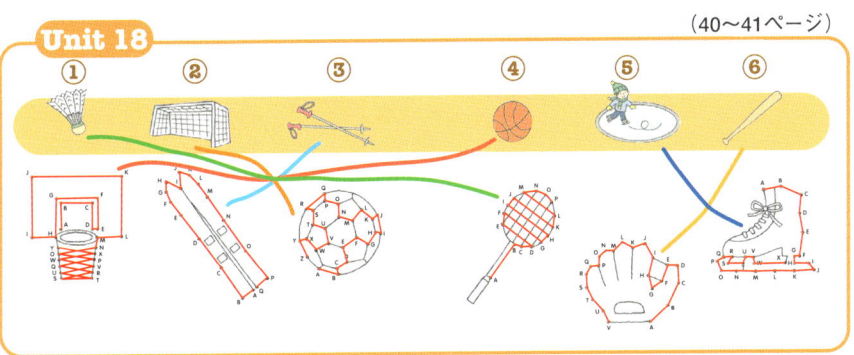

## Unit 17 (39ページ)

## Unit 19 (42～43ページ)

## Unit 20 (44ページ)

① rainy→sunny
② pasta→fish
③ 2+1=3→10+1=11
④ tulips→roses

## Unit 21 (46～47ページ)

(8:50) (9:00) (8:00) (7:30) (8:00) (8:00) (7:20) (4:00) (3:30) (12:00)

sixty-three 63

著者 ● 下 薫

英文校閲 ● Stephen Hubert

装丁・シリーズロゴデザイン ● 大薮胤美（フレーズ）

本文デザイン ● 河内沙耶花／桑沢祐子／馬場芽生（フレーズ）

装丁イラスト・キャラクターデザイン ● ハマダルコラ

本文イラスト ● ハマダルコラ／原ゆき／山本省三／佐古百美　すみもとななみ

CD制作 ● 東京オーディオ・ミュージックレコード株式会社

声の出演 ● Matt Lagan／Bianca Allen

音楽 ● すずきゆみ

編集・構成 ● 株式会社　童夢

## 下 薫（しも・かおる）
**Julie Kaoru Shimo**

ロサンゼルス生まれ。上智大学外国語学部卒業後、コロンビア大学大学院にて英語教授法、英語学を学ぶ。児童英語教育を言語習得理論、国際理解教育の観点から研究。小学校向け英語教育のカリキュラム開発、教材製作、教師研修などを行う。著書に『子どもを英語の達人に!!』（徳間文庫）、『はじめておぼえるえいごのたんご』（ジャパンタイムズ）、『キッズクラウン英和・和英辞典』（三省堂）がある。マジカルキッズ英語研究所代表。

## 英語のゲーム　音であそぼう

2005年 3月20日　第1刷発行
2022年 5月30日　第4刷発行

著　者 ● 下 薫
発行者 ● 株式会社三省堂　代表者　瀧本多加志
発行所 ● 株式会社三省堂
　　　　〒101-8371東京都千代田区神田三崎町2-22-14
　　　　電話　03-3230-9411（編集）　03-3230-9412（営業）
印刷所 ● 三省堂印刷株式会社
CD製作 ● 株式会社音研

落丁本・乱丁本はお取り替えいたします。
ISBN 978-4-385-36224-3　　　＜英語のゲーム・音・64pp.＞
©2005 Julie Kaoru Shimo/Sanseido Co., Ltd.　Printed in Japan

本書を無断で複写複製することは、著作権法上の例外を除き、禁じられています。また、本書を請負業者等の第三者に依頼してスキャン等によってデジタル化することは、たとえ個人や家庭内での利用であっても一切認められておりません。

| Unit<br>ユニット | Title<br>タイトル | Theme<br>テーマ<br>言語材料 | Linguistic Goals<br>言語学習目標<br>聞く、話す、読む、書く | Content Goals<br>Awareness<br>気づき学習<br>★Self-awareness<br>●Awareness of Others<br>▲Global Awareness | Songs & Chants<br>歌とチャンツ | Level<br>学習年齢 |
|---|---|---|---|---|---|---|
| 12 | The School Sugoroku<br>学校すごろくで遊ぼう | 学校<br>教科 | 教科が聞き取れ、言える。<br>クイズが聞き取れ、答えられる。 | ★自分の好きな科目を紹介できる。 | School Chant | 小学校中学年～ |
| 13 | Vacation Mix-Up<br>海や山で何して遊ぶ？ | レジャー<br>動作 | まとまった文が聞き取れ、言える。<br>動作、海や山に関する言葉が聞き取れ、言える。 | ★自信を持ってまとまった文章が言える。 | | |
| 14 | Friends & Feelings<br>気持ちをあらわす言葉 | 感情<br>体 | 感情表現が聞き取れ、言える。 | ▲日米の絵文字の違いが理解できる。<br>★自分が楽しい時、悲しい時の事を言える。<br>●友達の気持ちが理解できる。 | Let's Make a Face | |
| 15 | Homes of Wild Animals<br>動物たちのふるさと | 動物 | 世界の国と動物の名前が聞き取れ、言える。 | ▲世界の動物のふるさとを知り、野生動物について説明できる。 | | |
| 16 | Cooking Bingo<br>今日のごはんは何かな？ | 食べ物<br>料理 | 食べ物の名前が聞き取れ、言える。 | ★自分の好きな食べ物が言える。 | Food Chant | |
| 17 | Misa's Garden Story<br>庭で野菜ができるまで | 理科<br>植物<br>物語 | 動作を表す動詞が聞き取れ、言える。 | ▲植物の成長に必要な3要素がわかる。 | Oats, Peas, Beans, & Barley Grow<br>Story Chant | 小学校高学年～ |
| 18 | Sports Dot-to-Dot<br>スポーツ大好き | スポーツ<br>アルファベット | スポーツとその道具の名前が聞き取れ、言える。 | ★自分の好きなスポーツとその道具が言える。 | Cheerleading Chant | |
| 19 | Rhyming House<br>家の中でライミング | 家<br>家具 | 部屋と家具の名前、前置詞が聞き取れ、言える。 | ★自信を持ってライミングする単語や句を組み合わせ、リズム良く言える。 | On, In, Under Chant<br>Rhyming Chant | |
| 20 | Follow Your Dream<br>大人になったら何になる？ | 職業 | 職業に関する会話が聞き取れる。<br>絵の間違いが言える。 | ★将来の夢をはっきり言える。<br>●色々な職業に興味を持ち理解できる。 | | |
| 21 | Misa's One Fine Day<br>ミサの一日 | 一日のでき事<br>時間 | 時間と一日の行動を表す動詞が聞き取れる。<br>自分の行動が言える。 | ★自分の一日の行動を順序立てて言える。 | Can You Chant | |
| 22 | Storytelling<br>カエルの王子様 | 物語<br>ロールプレイ | 物語が聞き取れ、理解できる。<br>声に出してセリフが言える。 | ●友達と協力して劇ができる。<br>★自信を持ってロールプレーができる。 | | |

★Self-awareness…自分を知る　●Awareness of Others…他の人のことを知る　▲Global Awareness…地球全体のことを知る

# この本の構成

| Unit ユニット | Title タイトル | Theme テーマ 言語材料 | Linguistic Goals 言語学習目標 聞く、話す、読む、書く | Content Goals Awareness 気づき学習 ★Self-awareness ●Awareness of Others ▲Global Awareness | Songs & Chants 歌とチャンツ | Level 学習年齢 |
|---|---|---|---|---|---|---|
|  | **Nice to Meet You!** はじめまして！ | 自己紹介 名前 | 挨拶と自己紹介が聞き取れ、言える。 | ★自信を持って挨拶ができる。 ★自己紹介ができる。 |  | 幼児・小学校低学年〜 |
| 1 | **Alphabet Jingle & Chant** アルファベットでお口のたいそう | アルファベット | アルファベットの名前と音が聞き取れ、言える。 | ★自分の好きなものをチャンツではっきりと伝えられる。 | The ABC Song The ABC Jingle I Like Chant | |
| 2 | **Color Your Outfits** 洋服はどんな色？ | 洋服 色 | リズム良くチャンツが言える。 色、洋服の名前が聞き取れ、言える。 | ★自分が着ている洋服、好きな洋服を紹介できる。 | Mary is Wearing （替え歌） | |
| 3 | **This is My Family** ミサの家族しょうかい | 家族 形容詞 代名詞 | 家族の名前が聞き取れる。 家族の洋服について言える。 | ●自分の家族を自信を持って紹介できる。 | | |
| 4 | **Who Says Oink, Oink?** だれの鳴き声かな？ | ペット 家畜動物 数字 | ペット・家畜動物の名前が聞き取れ、言える。 | ★自分の飼っている（または飼いたい）ペットの事が言える。 | Old MacDonald Had a Farm | |
| 5 | **Fruits & Vegetables** くだものと野菜さがし | フルーツ 野菜 | 果物・野菜の名前が聞き取れ、言える。 | ★自分の好きな果物・野菜が言える。 | Fruit & Vegetable Chant | |
| 6 | **Numbers & Shapes Maze** 数字と形のめいろへようこそ | 数字 形 | 数字と形の名前が聞き取れ、言える。 | ★自分に関する数字が言える。 | Twinkle, Twinkle, Little Star | |
| 7 | **Jump Rope Rhymes** なわとび歌で遊ぼう | リズム 動作 | リズム良くチャンツが言える。 動作の表現が聞き取れ、動作をしながら言える。 | ★自分ができる事を自信を持って言える。 | ABC Soup I Love Coffee Teddy Bear | 小学校中学年〜 |
| 8 | **Toys Spot the Difference** クリスマスまちがいさがし | クリスマス | 絵の違いを表す英文が聞き取れる。 質問に答えられる。 | ★英語の質問に自信を持って答えられる。 | Jingle Bells | |
| 9 | **Shopping List Code** 買い物に行こう | 店 買い物 | 店や売っているものの名前が聞き取れ、言える。 | ★自分の好きな店と、そこで買いたいものが言える。 ●自分の町に興味を持ち紹介できる。 | I'm Going to the Store | |
| 10 | **Sing & Draw Vehicles** のりもの絵かき歌 | 乗り物 場所 | 乗り物と場所の名前が聞き取れ、言える。 | ★オリジナルの絵描き歌を想像力豊かに作れる。 | The Wheels on the Bus （替え歌） | |
| 11 | **Origami Newspaper** 新聞で折り紙をしよう | 動作 文化比較 | 帽子を作る動作を表す動詞が聞き取れ、言える。 | ▲外国文化に興味を持ち理解する。 ★日本の事を自信を持って紹介できる。 | | |